GROUNDBREAKERS

Albert Einstein

Struan Reid

Heinemann Library
Chicago, Illinois

Designed by AMR
Illustrated by Art Construction
Originated by Ambassador Litho
Printed in Hong Kong/China

05 04 03 02 01
10 9 8 7 6 5 4 3 2 1

Library of Congress Cataloging-in-Publication Data
Reid, Struan.
    Albert Einstein / Struan Reid.
    p. cm. – (Groundbreakers)
    Includes bibliographical references and index.
    Summary: traces the life and work of the famous physicist, from his childhood in
Germany and education in Switzerland through the development of his theories of
relativity to his campaign for peace after World War II.
    ISBN 1-57572-365-4 (lib. bdg.)   ISBN 1-58810-988-7 (pbk. bdg.)
    1. Einstein, Albert, 1879-1955—Juvenile literature. 2. Physicists—Biography—Juvenile
literature. [1. Einstein, Albert, 1879-1955. 2. Physicists.] I. Einstein, Albert, 1879-1955.
II. Title. II. Series.

    QC16.E5 R39 2000
    530'.092—dc21
    [B]   00-029591

Acknowledgments
The publishers would like to thank the following for permission to reproduce photographs:
Camera Press/Interfoto, p. 4; Mary Evans Picture Library, pp. 5, 35; AKG Photo, pp. 6, 7, 8, 11,
13, 15, 20, 21, 22, 23, 24, 28, 29, 30, 40; J. Allan Cash Ltd., pp. 9, 19; AKG Photo/Erich Lessing,
pp. 10, 18; Science Photo Library/Sheila Terry p. 12; Hulton Getty, pp. 14, 32, 36; Science Photo
Library/John Sanford, p. 25; Corbis/Bettmann, p. 31; Corbis, pp. 33, 34; Science Photo Library,
p. 37; Retrograph, p. 38; Camera Press/Alan Richards, p. 39; Science Photo Library/Fermilab,
p. 41; Science Photo Library/NASA, p. 43.

Our thanks to Patrick Fullick for his comments in the preparation of this book.

Some words are shown in bold, **like this.** You can find out what
they mean by looking in the glossary.

Contents

The Universe Explained

At first, Albert Einstein seems like the typical absent-minded professor—totally absorbed in his work and ignoring everyday concerns. With his baggy pants, wild white hair, and droopy moustache, he certainly looked the part. But he is also regarded by many as the greatest scientist of the 20th century, and that is why his face is instantly recognizable throughout the world.

New questions and surprising answers

Einstein is famous for his theories of relativity, which turned upside down scientists' beliefs about **gravity** and other scientific laws—laws that had been accepted for hundreds of years. Einstein's work changed people's understanding of the universe. His theories blew apart existing scientific beliefs and replaced them with answers to questions that had been puzzling scientists for centuries.

Einstein's first theory of relativity was published in 1905. The very next day, Einstein was being called a genius. He would remain famous for the rest of his life. He lived for another 50 years and wherever he went people flocked to see him, attracted by his fame.

"One of the greatest achievements in the history of human thought."

(A scientist in 1905, describing Einstein's first theory of relativity)

Albert Einstein's groundbreaking theories answered questions that had been puzzling scientists for centuries.

Revolutionary

Einstein's theories were so revolutionary that not everyone accepted them immediately. Most people found them extremely difficult to understand, and many still do today. They were aware that his work had opened up completely new ways of explaining the universe. However, while his discoveries gave many new answers, they also challenged long-held beliefs about topics such as time and space, which made some people feel very unsure. They began to wonder whether the universe has a beginning and what lies beyond. There had always been fixed answers to fixed questions, but now everything seemed to be in doubt.

Although Einstein's discoveries were beyond the understanding of many people, he had other strongly held beliefs that most people could understand—as a campaigner for world peace and a champion of truth and justice.

LA DOMENICA DEL CORRIERE

Supplemento settimanale illustrato del nuovo CORRIERE DELLA SERA - Abbonamenti: Italia, anno L. 1165, sem. L. 625 - Estero, anno L. 1765, sem. L. 925

Anno 52 — N. 3   15 Gennaio 1950   L. 25,—

Le formule misteriose del "mago,,: Alberto Einstein, creatore della teoria della relatività che ha aperto la via all'utilizzazione dell'energia atomica, ha enunciato nei giorni scorsi, in una lezione tenuta a Princeton, una nuova geniale teoria sulla concezione dell'universo (vedi altre notizie a pag. 4).

Einstein's face was recognized throughout the world. Here he appears on the cover of an Italian magazine of 1950.

In Charlie Chaplin's words:

"The people are applauding you because none of them understands you, and applauding me because everybody understands me."

(Reported to have been said to Einstein by the comedian Charlie Chaplin when driving in a car with him)

Early Life

Albert Einstein was born on March 14, 1879 in the southern German town of Ulm. He was the first child and only son of Hermann and Pauline Einstein. Their new baby boy had an unusual-shaped head and an overweight body, and when Pauline's mother, Jette Koch, saw her new grandson, she cried out: "Much too fat! Much too fat!" A doctor reassured Albert's parents that their son would develop normally, and within a few months his body had grown to a proper size, but the back of his skull would always be an odd shape.

Hidden talents

Einstein's father, Hermann, was an electrical engineer with a small electrochemical factory in Ulm. But his business was not doing well, and when Albert was just one year old, he moved with his family from Ulm to the nearby city of Munich. There, Hermann went into business with his brother Jacob, making electrical instruments and equipment. The family shared a large, comfortable house with Jacob on the edge of the city. But Hermann was never a successful businessman.

Albert was taught at home until he was seven years old. Then he went to school, but he did not stand out. He was quiet and shy and never enjoyed sports, preferring to sit alone and read.

Hermann and Pauline Einstein created a warm, friendly home for their children, Albert and his sister Maja, who was two and a half years younger. Pauline was a talented musician, and she gave Albert violin lessons. These instilled a love of music in him that would remain with him for the rest of his life, giving him peace and enjoyment. The Einsteins were Jewish, but they never followed the Jewish religious customs. However, Albert always believed in the idea that there might be some "other power" much greater than humans.

Albert's quiet, reserved exterior hid an inquisitive and determined mind. While he was growing up, many new scientific discoveries and mechanical inventions were being made. Albert was developing interests of his own, especially in **algebra.** He was encouraged by his uncle Jacob and by a young student named Max Talmud, whom Albert's parents had befriended. He lent young Albert books on science and philosophy.

This photograph of the Einstein children was taken in 1884, when the family was living in Munich. Albert was five and Maja was two and a half.

Pauline Einstein

Pauline Einstein was the daughter of Julius Koch, a baker from Cannstatt in Germany who had made a fortune in the grain trade. She was intensely proud of her two children and encouraged them to work hard. She believed strongly in the education of women and was overjoyed when her daughter Maja later earned a university degree in languages. At that time it was still unusual for women to continue their education beyond high school.

A New Nationality

In 1894, the Einstein family business collapsed and Albert's parents and sister moved to Milan in Italy—business prospects looked more promising there. Albert, now 15 years old, was left behind to complete his school education in Munich. He hated being separated from his family and in the following year, 1895, he left Munich and joined his family in Milan.

Disappointment into triumph

Hermann and Pauline were disappointed and angry that their son had dropped out of school before finishing his courses. Hermann wanted his son to get a decent job, probably in electrical engineering. But Albert was determined to be a philosophy teacher, even though he had spoiled his chances of earning a place at a university by leaving school early. His father finally persuaded him to study for something more practical. Albert applied for a course in electrical engineering at the Institute of Technology in Zurich, Switzerland—a college with an international reputation.

Albert studied hard for the entrance examination to the Zurich Institute. When he was not studying, he helped out in the new electrical business his family had started in Milan. But his parents were surprised and shocked when, in 1895, Albert failed the exam. He received high scores in mathematics and **physics,** but he failed badly in subjects that did not interest him, such as French, chemistry, and biology.

Despite this failure, however, the staff at the Institute were so impressed by his mathematics and physics grades that they suggested he try the exam again. Therefore, at the age of 16, Albert went to study for a year at a school in Aarau, a small town 25 miles (40 kilometers) west of Zurich.

Young Albert Einstein studied at the Institute of Technology in Zurich, Switzerland, from 1896 until 1900.

Albert got excellent grades and was awarded a diploma in 1896 that entitled him to enroll directly at the Zurich Institute, without having to take the entrance examination again. The same year, he gave up his German citizenship—he felt more at home in Switzerland and was planning to apply for Swiss nationality.

Zurich today is a thriving modern city.

Fresh start

Albert now began a four-year course at the Zurich Institute, to become a teacher of mathematics and physics. However, he found the course boring and did not always attend the lectures. He was disappointed that the lecturers seemed to ignore the latest scientific developments.

Albert made a number of close friends at the Institute. They discussed mathematics, attended concerts, and enjoyed each other's company. Two of these friends in particular, Marcel Grossman and Angelo Besso, remained close to Albert for the rest of their lives. But he still took little interest in his work. However, Grossman lent him his own lecture notes and, with his help, Albert graduated in August 1900 with top grades. The following year, at the age of 22, he was finally granted Swiss citizenship.

"You are a smart boy, Einstein, a very smart boy. But you have one great fault: you do not let yourself be told anything."

(Heinrich Weber, Professor of Physics at the Zurich Institute)

Mileva Maric

Mileva Maric was also studying science and mathematics at the Institute while Albert was there. She was the only woman in his class—at that time, very few women went on to study at universities. Mileva came from Bacska in what is now Serbia. Albert became very friendly with her and they would eventually marry. But his friends and family were surprised at his interest in her—she was four years older than him and seemed to have little sense of humor.

Early Career

Albert Einstein was now qualified as a mathematics and **physics** teacher. He was eager to start work as a lecturer, but he found it very hard to find any work at all. His disagreements with his lecturers at the Institute meant that he had little chance of getting a job there.

Signs of promise

Einstein eventually found some work as a temporary schoolteacher in Switzerland, first in a town called Winterthur and then in the capital city of Bern. He loved the work and got great satisfaction from sharing his knowledge with his students. When he was not teaching, he continued with his own research in physics and also started writing articles for scientific journals. This enabled him to publish his ideas on some of the scientific mysteries of the day—ideas that would astound the world a few years later.

However, Einstein was becoming frustrated. He felt that his career plans were being blocked wherever he looked. But once again his friend from his student days, Marcel Grossmann, came to his aid. Marcel's father was very influential in Switzerland and recommended Einstein for a job in the **Patent** Office in Bern. He was accepted.

On June 23, 1902, Einstein began his new job as a Technical Expert (Third Class) in the Bern Patent Office. He was a low-grade clerk, part of a team of twelve, and his work involved inspecting and registering applications for patents from Swiss inventors. Many people would have found the work dull and repetitive, but Einstein enjoyed it. His work hours also allowed him to continue with his own interests and research. He was still writing and publishing scientific papers.

Albert Einstein's desk at the Patent Office in Bern, where he worked on the theory of relativity, has been preserved.

Marriage

With a secure job and a regular income, Einstein was now in a position to get married. He and Mileva had been seeing a lot of each other and they shared many interests, particularly their love of mathematics. But Einstein's parents, especially his mother, were against the relationship—they had never liked Mileva. In fact, Pauline Einstein believed that Mileva must have cast a spell over her son! Despite this opposition from Einstein's family, he and Mileva were married on January 6, 1903. He was 23 years old and she was 27. They had three children. The first, a girl named Lieserl, was born in 1903, before they were married, and was later adopted by another family. She was followed by two boys: Hans Albert, born in 1904; and Eduard, born in 1910.

Albert and Mileva Einstein posed with their baby son Hans Albert in 1904. He was their second child.

The Olympia Academy

During the same period, Einstein and some of his friends met regularly in each other's houses and went on hiking trips together. They called themselves "The Olympia Academy." They discussed the latest scientific research, philosophy, and literature. "Our means were frugal [poor] but our joy was boundless," one of the group, Maurice Solovine, later wrote.

Motion, Distance, and Time

The theories of Sir Isaac Newton, one of the world's greatest scientists, dominated **physics** *until 1905.*

Until the end of the 19th century, most **physicists** based their work on the theories of the famous English scientist Sir Isaac Newton (1642–1727). In 1687, Newton published a very influential book entitled *The Mathematical Principles of Natural Philosophy*, usually known by its shortened Latin name of the *Principia*. This work included his three Laws of Motion, which are rules that relate force and **gravity** and explain the principles that underlie the movement of all objects, on Earth and in space.

Questions ...

Newton's Laws of Motion have had a major influence on scientific thinking. But in the early 20th century, scientists began to ask new questions that these laws could not answer fully. For example, if everything is constantly moving, as Newton's laws claim, how is it possible to measure exact distances between objects and the exact time between events?

... and answers

The work of two American scientists, Edward Morley (1838–1923) and Albert Michelson (1852–1931), provided a partial answer to this question. In 1887, they performed an experiment to measure the speed of light. They thought that if they were able to measure this, then they would have a fixed point against which other distances and events could be measured.

Morley and Michelson based their experiment on the work of a 19th-century Scottish scientist named James Clerk Maxwell. He believed that light was a form of **electromagnetic wave** that traveled through a mysterious light-carrying substance called the "ether" that filled the whole of space. Morley and Michelson suggested that it should be possible to detect differences in the speed of light in different directions as the earth was moving through the ether.

They reflected beams of light from mirrors, so that some of the light traveled in the same direction as the earth was moving in, and some traveled at right angles to this direction. They measured how long light took to travel in each direction and checked their results by rotating the apparatus to change the direction in which each beam of light traveled.

Shock wave

However, Morley and Michelson could detect no differences in the speed of light. Instead, the speed of light appeared to be the same in whatever direction they measured it. This result shook the scientific world because it showed that while Newton's ideas explained movement on Earth, they could not be applied to the whole universe. Eighteen years later, Albert Einstein was able to explain exactly what was happening.

In his experiments with Edward Morley, Albert Michelson raised questions about the speed of light that were answered eighteen years later by Einstein's special theory of relativity.

Einstein's Year of Miracles

Although still a young man, Einstein's work—especially his three famous papers of 1905—made him world-famous in scientific circles.

The first few years of Einstein's marriage were happy and contented. In 1905, a year that became known as his year of miracles, he published three new scientific papers, all of which had great impact. "Ideas come from God," said Einstein.

Atoms and photons

One of Einstein's papers discussed the movement of tiny **particles** known as **atoms.** Until then, many scientists were uncertain whether atoms really existed. Nearly 80 years earlier, in 1827, the **botanist** Robert Brown noted that dust particles on the surface of water are always moving in all directions. This movement of particles came to be known as *Brownian motion*, even though Brown was unable to explain why it was happening.

ROBERT BROWN

Robert Brown (1773–1858) was a Scottish botanist who carried out many studies with a microscope. He collected 4000 plant **species** and spent five years classifying them. In 1827, the year that he discovered Brownian motion, he became keeper of the new botanical department at the British Museum.

Using mathematical equations, Einstein showed that the **molecules** in a liquid bump into the dust particles on the surface, making the particles move quickly, as if alive.

Three years later, in 1908, the French scientist Jean Perrin made detailed studies of Brownian motion. He studied the movement of particles in water and his results showed that Einstein's mathematical equations had been correct. Perrin's experiments provided the first evidence that atoms and molecules really do exist.

Einstein's second paper of 1905 contained his ideas about the energy from light turning into electrical energy. He said that light consisted of tiny "packets" of energy, which he called *photons*. Adapting an idea first developed in 1900 by the German scientist Max Planck, he showed that when light shines onto a metal surface, light photons knock **electrons** out of the metal atoms, which produces an electric current. This is known as the *photoelectric effect*.

Max Planck, the German scientist who had a major influence on physics, was Professor of Physics at various times at universities in Kiel, Berlin, and Munich.

MAX PLANCK

Max Planck (1858–1947) was born in Kiel, Germany. He studied **physics** at Munich University, where he later became a professor. In 1900, he published a scientific paper that introduced the idea of "quantizing energy." This stated that energy, such as light, was not continuous. Instead, energy existed in the form of tiny units that he called *quanta*. This idea led to the development of **quantum mechanics,** a new set of laws describing how atomic particles behave. In 1919, Planck was awarded the **Nobel prize** for physics for his discovery that energy is quantized.

Relativity

Of the three scientific papers Einstein published in 1905, the most astounding of all was the one on his special theory of relativity. It is known as "special" because it applies only to certain special conditions. It was published in June and contained Einstein's explanation for the baffling results from Morley and Michelson's 1887 light experiment. It rocked the scientific world because it completely overturned Newton's view of fixed measurements of time and motion.

What is it?

In the special theory of relativity, Einstein showed that all movement is relative—all we can measure is how fast we are moving in relation to something else. Although the mathematical details of the special theory of relativity are extremely complicated, the main idea can be explained quite simply.

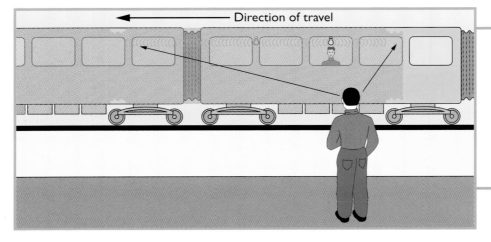

← Direction of travel

This diagram illustrates Einstein's special theory of relativity, which showed there is no universal, absolute time.

Imagine that a train is pulling out from a station. A flashing light bulb is hanging from the ceiling in the exact center of the carriage. It sends out two flashes of light at exactly the same time but in opposite directions. If you were inside the carriage, you would see the light flashes reach the two ends of the carriage at exactly the same time. But if you were standing on the station platform, you would see something different as the train passes by. From the platform, the speed of both flashes of light is exactly the same as the light speed that you measure inside the train. However, as the light moves outwards from the bulb, the train is moving forwards.

From the platform, you would see the flash of light that is moving backwards hit the back wall of the carriage before seeing the forward-moving flash hit the front wall.

The speed of light is constant for all observers, at whatever speed they are traveling. But this example shows that an event—in this case the two light flashes hitting the end walls of the carriage—that one observer sees happen at exactly the same time, another observer (who is moving relative to the first observer) sees happen at different times.

With the special theory of relativity, Einstein showed that there is no universal, absolute time. Time, like motion, is relative to the observer. The only constant is the speed of light.

TIME PASSES SLOWLY

As well as overturning Newton's idea of absolute time, the special theory of relativity predicted that the faster anything travels, the more slowly time will pass. For example, if an astronaut travels into space at nearly the speed of light, time will pass more slowly for the astronaut than for his or her twin back on Earth. When the astronaut returns to Earth, he or she will not be as old as the twin left behind on Earth.

The Famous Professor

Following the publication of these amazing scientific papers, Einstein's name slowly became known to many scientists of the time. One of the first to show an interest in his work was Max Planck himself, who wrote asking for more information on the special theory of relativity. Einstein's old mathematics teacher from Zurich, Professor Hermann Minkowski, also took an interest in the theory. But while some scientists agreed with Einstein's work, many others dismissed it as nonsense.

Einstein's laboratory at the University of Zurich was cluttered with wires and scientific instruments.

Offers of work

In spite of growing interest in his scientific work, Einstein stayed in his job at the Bern **Patent** Office and was promoted to the position of Technical Expert (Second Class). He remained in this job for another five years. In 1908, he began teaching part-time at the University of Bern. Finally, in 1909, he resigned from the Patent Office at the age of 30.

HERMANN MINKOWSKI

The German mathematician Hermann Minkowski (1864–1909) had been Einstein's mathematics professor at the Zurich Institute. Like many of Einstein's teachers there, he had clashed with the young student. However, it was he who developed Einstein's special theory of relativity. In 1908, he suggested that there are not three dimensions, but four—three dimensions in space and a fourth dimension in time. Einstein would later build upon this idea of space-time to develop his general theory of relativity in 1915.

The city of Prague, on the banks of the Vltava River, was Einstein's home for about a year, while he served as Professor of Physics at the university there.

He took up a permanent teaching position at the University of Zurich, but his lectures were never well attended—his teaching methods seemed very dull to the students. Einstein found it difficult to convey complex ideas in an interesting way. However, the importance of his discoveries was now beginning to be recognized and offers of work from universities all over Europe came pouring in.

In 1911, Einstein was appointed Professor of **Physics** at the University of Prague, the capital of the present-day Czech Republic. With this new job came a good salary, and Einstein and his family moved into a comfortable new apartment in Prague. Einstein's new work gave him access to the huge university libraries with their books and information on all the latest scientific discoveries. He was also in regular contact with many of the most important scientists of the day.

Hermann Minkowski was so impressed by Einstein's work that in 1907 he wrote:

"From now on space and time separately have vanished into the merest shadows, and only a sort of combination of the two preserves any reality."

By this, Minkowski meant that the measurements of space and time could never be the same again.

Back to Germany

Einstein enjoyed talking over his ideas with his fellow scientists. He felt that he did his best work when his relationships with other people were going well.

The Einsteins were never very happy in Prague. They were there only about a year before they moved back to Zurich, where Einstein was appointed Professor of **Physics** at his old college, the Zurich Institute. He was 33 years old and 17 years had passed since, as a boy of 16, he had first failed the entrance examination to the college. Mileva was happier to be back in Zurich, because they were among their old friends once more. One of these was Marcel Grossmann, who began helping Einstein to develop his work on the relativity theory. Einstein wrote at the time about this work: "I occupy myself exclusively with the problem."

Losing his family

Einstein stayed in Zurich for two years. In December 1913, he was offered a good job at the University of Berlin in Germany, as the Research Director at the new Institute of Physics. This was a very exciting offer—it was an extremely important post and would provide Einstein with the ideal conditions for completing his work on relativity.

Einstein started working in Berlin in the spring of 1914. In April, Mileva and their two sons, Hans Albert and Eduard, joined him. But no sooner had they arrived than Mileva took them back to Zurich. She disliked living in Germany, and being in Berlin would mean that they were closer to her mother-in-law, Pauline Einstein, who had never liked her. Einstein was very upset by their departure. However, for some time he and Mileva had been very unhappy together, and it was now obvious that their marriage was coming to an end.

Mileva and the two boys moved into a rented apartment in Zurich, and Mileva had to give piano and mathematics lessons to help pay the rent. Although he was separated from his sons, Einstein was happy in Berlin and could now concentrate on his work. He later described Berlin as the place he "felt closely connected to by human and scientific relations."

Mileva's contribution

Since first meeting as students in Zurich, Mileva had been a valuable source of support and information for her husband's work. They spent many hours together discussing their ideas. When Einstein won the 1921 **Nobel prize** for physics, he gave the prize money ($35,000) to Mileva to support herself and their sons. But Mileva became very bitter and claimed much of the credit for Einstein's success. She was no doubt a great help to Einstein in the early years of their marriage, but how much she contributed directly to his work is unknown.

In this German poster from World War One, the government appeals to the German people's national pride and family values.

When Einstein moved back to Germany, the country of his birth, at the beginning of 1914, his prospects looked promising. But the storm clouds were already gathering—one of the most destructive wars ever to be fought would soon explode across the face of Europe.

A world gone mad

On August 1, 1914, World War One broke out between Germany, Austria, and their allies on one side, and Britain, France, Russia, and their allies on the other. Many people on both sides greeted the outbreak of war with enthusiasm—they believed that they would be fighting for freedom and justice. But Einstein believed that the war was unnecessary and, indeed, was sheer destructive madness. He was especially angered by the work of the scientists who invented terrible new weapons, such as poisonous gas. He believed this was an abuse of science.

A year after the outbreak of war, Einstein signed a document called the Manifesto to Europeans, along with many other famous people in Germany and elsewhere. This was an appeal to everyone who valued "the culture of Europe" to come to their senses and form an association of countries.

This "league of nations" would be dedicated to the promotion of peace between nations. By signing this manifesto, Einstein publicly declared himself to be a **pacifist.** From now on until his death, he would actively support peaceful actions to settle disputes, as well as campaign for justice and tolerance. At the same time, Einstein joined a political party that tried to end the war. It was banned by the German government in 1916.

Some time away

In the summer of 1915, Einstein went on a vacation to a remote island in the Baltic Sea. He followed this trip with a visit to his sons in Zurich, and he took Hans Albert walking and boating in southern Germany.

Before returning to Berlin, Einstein visited Romain Rolland, a French writer and fellow pacifist who lived near Lake Geneva in Switzerland.

In a fellow pacifist's words:

"He [Einstein] is very much alive and fond of laughter. He cannot help giving an amusing twist to the most serious thoughts…He is one of the very few men whose spirit had remained free among the general servility."

(The pacifist Romain Rolland, after meeting Einstein on September 6, 1915)

Einstein was outraged by the Germans' use of poisonous gases in the trenches of World War One.

23

Reaching the Goal

While he was campaigning for peace and becoming involved in political issues, Einstein continued with his scientific research. During the war years, from 1914 until 1918, he wrote over 50 scientific papers and published a book. He was also becoming increasingly famous and, wherever he went, crowds turned out to greet him. Switzerland remained **neutral** throughout the war, and Einstein's Swiss passport meant that he could travel, despite the war. He visited other scientists and **pacifists** in Switzerland and the Netherlands. He was invited to address scientific meetings and, at last, more scientists were beginning to take his ideas seriously.

Too little time

During the autumn of 1915, Einstein missed meals and worked late into the night. When he did eat, he cooked everything together in the same pot to save time and trouble. One day, his future stepdaughter Margot found him boiling an egg in some soup, planning to eat both! His health suffered as a result of these bad eating habits, but as always his work came first and he continued with his research.

While he was living in Berlin, Einstein was taken care of by his cousin Elsa and her daughter Margot (right).

Gradually, Einstein came closer and closer to his goal. At the end of November 1915, he finally worked out the answer he had been searching for since ten years earlier. At last, he had discovered how to include the effects of **gravity** in the relativity theory. It was as if he had been feeling his way through darkness and had suddenly come out into brilliant sunshine.

A new beginning

The general theory of relativity completely changed the way in which we understand the world. For 200 years, many of the most important problems in **physics** had been explained using Newton's laws. The general theory now replaced Newton's work. It provided a revolutionary new means to explore and understand our universe, explaining its origin and destiny.

Some people were alarmed by these discoveries—they felt that they could not even rely on the evidence of their own eyes any more. But others were excited and felt inspired by feelings of awe and wonder at the fantastic laws of nature that Einstein had revealed. His discoveries also had a great effect on the work of writers, artists, and philosophers.

Einstein's general theory of relativity, published in 1916, explained many of the mysteries of the universe.

In March 1916, Einstein published his general theory of relativity. His friend, the **physicist** Max Born, described this as

"a great work of art...the greatest feat of human thinking about nature."

The General Theory of Relativity

Like the special theory of relativity, Einstein's general theory of relativity is extremely complicated. But we can explain the main ideas contained in this theory quite simply.

In the general theory of relativity, Einstein writes that space is warped or "curved" by objects and that the more massive the object, the greater this effect is. The extent of this warping or curvature of space is greatest near the object and becomes progressively less as the distance from the object increases.

Imagine space as a flat rubber sheet. If a heavy rock is placed in the center of the sheet, the rubber will warp or sag in the middle. The heavier the rock, the greater the sag. If a small ball is rolled across the rubber sheet, it will go down the slope towards the rock. The closer it gets to the rock, the more the ball will be pulled down towards it. If it passes very close to the rock, the ball will circle, or orbit, the rock repeatedly. In the same way, **radiation** and material objects are pulled in by the curvature of space near massive objects. That is why the earth orbits the sun, and the moon orbits the earth.

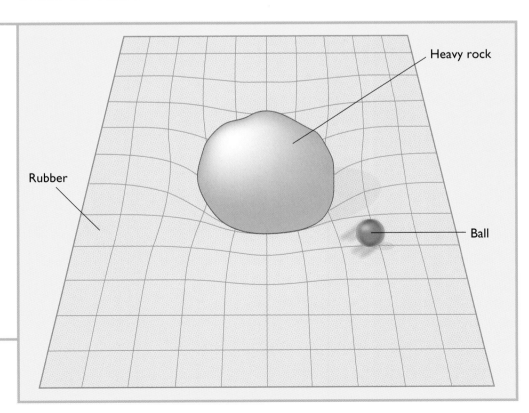

This diagram explains the general theory of relativity. Space is the most warped closest to the most massive object, where the gravitational pull is greatest. Smaller objects are attracted by this pull.

Heavy rock

Rubber

Ball

The general theory of relativity also states that light has **mass** and would therefore be affected by **gravity.** For example, starlight passing close to the sun will be pulled towards the sun, following the curvature in space caused by the sun's mass. Einstein hoped that astronomers would be able to test this theory.

Proving the theory

Einstein published his general theory in 1916. An opportunity to test it arose three years later, in 1919, when there was an eclipse of the sun. The bending of light by gravity that Einstein predicted was detected by photographing two stars during the eclipse. A team of astronomers, led by an English **physicist** named Arthur Eddington, measured the position of the stars. As the light rays from the stars passed the sun, they were "bent" by its field of gravity. As a result, to the astronomers the two stars appeared to be further apart than usual.

This diagram shows how gravity bends light. The path of the starlight is bent by the sun's gravity, making the stars appear to be farther apart than they actually are.

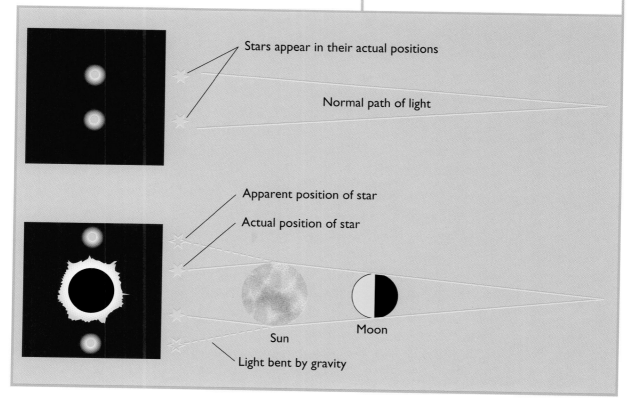

Stars appear in their actual positions

Normal path of light

Apparent position of star

Actual position of star

Sun

Moon

Light bent by gravity

The year 1916, in which Einstein published his general theory of relativity, also marked the end of the period of his greatest work. He had been working extremely hard—in just one year he had produced ten scientific papers and a book that explained relativity—and he was exhausted. His marriage had broken down completely and the separation from his sons upset him. In 1917, Einstein fell seriously ill with a stomach ulcer. Weak and in great pain, he spent much of his time in bed. But even then he would work non-stop for long stretches.

Einstein and his cousin Elsa Lowenthal were married in 1919, five years after he moved to Berlin. They would remain together until Elsa's death in 1936.

New battles

Since moving to Berlin in 1914, Einstein had developed a close relationship with his cousin, Elsa Lowenthal. She persuaded him to move to an apartment near hers. Visiting him every day, she helped him back to health, cooking his meals and making sure that he kept to a strict diet. Elsa was divorced from her first husband and had two daughters. In February 1919, Einstein and Mileva were finally divorced, and in the following June he married Elsa. They were together for seventeen years, until Elsa's death in 1936.

Einstein may have been more settled now in his home life, but this was a time of great unrest in Europe, especially in Germany. World War One ended on November 11, 1918 with the surrender of Germany. But the fighting continued on the streets in Germany as the people battled among themselves for control of the country.

Enemies of the state

Following Germany's defeat in World War One, many Germans looked around for people to blame. They blamed the newly-formed and more free-thinking **Weimar Republic,** which they referred to as "the Traitor Republic." They also blamed the **pacifists** and Jews. People were denounced as "traitors" if they had been pacifists during the war. As a Jew, Einstein also became the target of **anti-Semitic** Germans, who were angered by his campaign for peace and irritated by his growing fame throughout the world. He was also attacked by some of his German scientist colleagues. They were led by a **physicist** named Philipp Lenard, who talked about "German **physics"** and criticized "Jewish science." He denounced Einstein as a supporter of peace, a **socialist,** and a Jew.

Einstein enjoyed boating, and some of his happiest and most relaxing moments were when he was able to get away from his work and sail on lakes.

German scientists were generally unwelcome at scientific meetings after the end of World War One. However, as a well-known supporter of peace, Einstein was welcomed wherever he went, and he was invited to give lectures throughout Europe. Finally, in 1922, Einstein was awarded the 1921 **Nobel prize** for physics. However, this was not for his work on relativity. It was for his less important work on the photoelectric effect, which he had published in 1905.

A Growing Public Role

During the 1920s, Einstein continued to give lectures around the world. As hostility towards him increased in Germany, he welcomed these trips abroad, and wherever he and Elsa went, the lecture halls were crowded with people. He received enthusiastic reports in newspapers and he was appointed guest lecturer at universities throughout the world.

The French newspaper *L'Humanité*, reporting on Einstein's visit to France, said:

"Everyone had the impression of being in the presence of a sublime genius."

Science moves on

Einstein was also world-famous because of his views on politics and peace. The League of Nations had been founded in 1920 to try and maintain peace between nations, and in 1922, Einstein became a member of the League's Committee on Intellectual Cooperation. In 1925, he campaigned for the ending of mandatory military service.

*By the time this photograph of Einstein and fellow **pacifists** was taken in Berlin in 1923, he was becoming more and more involved in the campaign for world peace and disarmament.*

Niels Bohr's work on quantum mechanics would lead to many disagreements with Einstein, but they always remained close friends.

Einstein also supported the Women's International League for Peace and Freedom, which called for international **disarmament.**

With his own, most important work behind him, Einstein now became involved in two other areas of **physics**—the unified field theory and **quantum mechanics.** But towards the end of the 1920s, his ideas were being overtaken by new research. Quantum mechanics describes the behavior of the **particles** of **matter** that make up atoms—protons, neutrons, and **electrons.** A number of new discoveries, notably by the New Zealand **physicist** Ernest Rutherford and the Danish physicist Niels Bohr, suggested that these particles behave randomly, by chance. This uncertainty contradicted everything that had been believed so far and Einstein could not accept it. "God does not play dice," he said. However, other leading physicists were beginning to accept the idea of chance, and even though his scientific reputation was untouchable, Einstein became increasingly isolated from new developments.

NIELS BOHR

Niels Bohr (1885–1962) was born in Denmark, the son of a professor of **physiology.** By 1913, he had devised a new model of the structure of the atom, using the ideas of quantum mechanics. He showed that electrons move around the **nucleus** of the atom in different levels of set amounts of energy, sometimes called "shells." He won the 1922 **Nobel prize** for physics, the year after Einstein. He was against **Fascism** and when the Germans invaded Denmark in 1940, he escaped by boat to Sweden and then to the United States.

Life Changes

Throughout the 1920s and into the early '30s, Einstein continued his campaign for world peace. In written articles and public lectures, he called on people to refuse to serve in their country's army, to stop producing weapons, and to work for peace instead.

Nazi rallies marching through the streets were a common sight in Berlin during the 1930s. The Nazi Party encouraged hatred towards anyone they regarded as enemies of Germany. The figure standing in the car is Adolf Hitler.

The politics of hate

At the same time as Einstein was calling for peace, a terrifying new character was emerging on the world stage—Adolf Hitler. He was supported by various groups of people in Germany who attacked anyone they regarded as enemies of their own distorted views of German patriotism.

These included religious leaders, scientists, artists, and philosophers. They also whipped up anti-Jewish hysteria.

In 1933, Adolf Hitler and his **Nazi** Party came to power in Germany. Einstein and Elsa were visiting the United States at the time. In Einstein's absence, his scientific writings were attacked for being "Jewish" and therefore un-German. His books were publicly burned, along with the works of other Jews, **pacifists,** and anti-Nazis. Several peace campaigners were arrested and even imprisoned. Einstein's name was published on the first page of a list of "enemies" of Germany.

ZIONISM

With the increasing hostility shown to Jews in 1930s Germany and elsewhere in Europe, Einstein became involved in a movement called **Zionism.** Zionists were people who supported the claims of Jews to establish a Jewish homeland in the Middle East. This eventually happened in 1948, when the state of Israel was founded, displacing many thousands of native Palestinian people from their homeland. For the rest of his life, Einstein helped Jewish people in need and encouraged the teaching of science in the new state of Israel.

Einstein emigrates

Realizing that his life was in danger, Einstein decided not to return to Germany. He stayed for a few months in Belgium and then England. On October 17, 1933, he and Elsa left Europe for a new life in the United States. Like many other Jews, he never returned to Germany. The previous year, in 1932, Princeton University in New Jersey had offered Einstein the position of Professor of **Physics** at the **Institute for Advanced Study.** By the end of that year, he had made up his mind to accept, and from 1933 until his death 22 years later, Princeton was his home.

In Einstein's words:

"In the last analysis, everyone is a human being, irrespective of whether he is an American or a German, a Jew or a Gentile [non-Jew]. If it were possible to manage with this point of view, which is the only dignified one, I would be a happy man."

(In a letter to the *New York Herald Tribune* newspaper in 1935)

The Heart of the Atom

The American physicist J. Robert Oppenheimer (1904–67) was director of the Los Alamos laboratory from 1943 to 1945. It was here that the first atomic bomb was produced. He later opposed the development of the hydrogen ("H") bomb.

In Einstein's words

Einstein believed that the Nazis had to be stopped and if this meant war, then it was unavoidable. He wrote:

"Organized power can be opposed only by organized power. Much as I regret this, there is no other way."

The growing menace from **Nazi** Germany, combined with the attacks on German Jews and anyone else opposed to Nazi beliefs, eventually convinced Einstein that at certain times war is necessary to stop aggression. He still clung to his ideals of world peace but saw that for now this was not possible. However, he would soon be involved with the most destructive weapon in history.

A world dilemma

When World War Two broke out in 1939, Einstein and other scientists wrote to President Franklin D. Roosevelt, urging him to begin development of an atomic bomb. Einstein knew that German scientists had discovered that huge amounts of energy were released by splitting **atoms.** He was afraid that they would draw upon this knowledge and build an atomic bomb first.

Albert Einstein did not invent the atomic bomb, but it was his $E = mc^2$ equation of 1905 that stated the basic principle of the bomb. When the United States entered the war in 1941, President Roosevelt set up what was called the Manhattan Project to develop an atomic bomb, following the advice of Einstein and other scientists.

Enrico Fermi (1901–54) was the greatest Italian scientist of the 20th century. He studied at the University of Pisa and in 1938, as an opponent of **Fascism,** he left for the U.S., where he worked at Columbia University in New York. In 1942, he produced the first controlled nuclear reaction. Although he was involved in the development of the first atomic bombs, he opposed American plans to build another, more powerful bomb known as the hydrogen or "H" bomb.

By the time war broke out, German scientists had discovered that if the **nucleus** of an atom was split in two, in a process called *nuclear fission*, an enormous amount of energy was released. If this energy were uncontrolled, there would be a massive explosion. In 1942, the Italian scientist Enrico Fermi built a device called a nuclear reactor in which he produced controlled **nuclear energy.**

*Enrico Fermi, who left Italy for the United States in protest against the policies of the Fascist government of Benito Mussolini, was awarded the **Nobel prize** for **physics** in 1938.*

Japan

The first atomic bombs were developed under the supervision of American **physicist** J. Robert Oppenheimer, who was in charge of the Manhattan Project. By the time they were close to being ready for use, the war with Germany was coming to an end. Einstein wrote another letter to President Roosevelt, urging him not to use the bombs. But the war with the Japanese still continued. After Roosevelt's death in April, Harry S. Truman became president. In August 1945, believing that little else could persuade the Japanese to surrender, the U.S. dropped two bombs on the Japanese cities of Hiroshima and Nagasaki. Tens of thousands of people were killed instantly, and many thousands more died slowly and painfully later from the effects of the bombs.

After the War

Once the war was over, Einstein returned to his campaign for peace and called even more vigorously for nuclear **disarmament.** "The war is won," he said, "but the peace is not." He realized the dangers that this new nuclear power posed. He had lived through two terrible world wars and was sickened by the mindless destruction they had caused.

New dangers

Einstein stepped up his campaign for peace, in letters, interviews, radio broadcasts, and public speeches. He believed that a new world government should be created that would finally put an end to the rivalry between nations. He believed that this was the only answer for a world that was now on the brink of destruction by nuclear warfare. He wrote: "Science has brought forth this danger but the real problem is in the hearts and minds of men."

Einstein believed that while the huge amount of energy created by nuclear power should not be used for destructive purposes, it could be used to help the world. But even here, Einstein saw the dangers and warned that new science-based technology should be kept under very strict control in order to avoid the destruction of the world.

In Einstein's words:

"All our…technological progress—our very civilization—is like an axe in the hand of a pathological criminal."

(In a letter to a friend in 1917)

Einstein swears the oath of allegiance as he becomes a U.S. citizen in 1940.

Physicists Otto Hahn and Lise Meitner worked together in Berlin during the 1930s, until Meitner left Germany for Sweden.

These years after the war also brought family concerns to Einstein. For many years his youngest son Eduard had been mentally ill. Mileva was now also very ill and Einstein was receiving upsetting news about her and their son. He had always kept the promise he had made 25 years earlier to care for them financially, and he sent her regular payments. These helped to pay for Eduard's expensive medical bills. Einstein had last seen his son in May 1933, and they would never meet again. Eduard died in a psychiatric hospital in Switzerland in 1962, where he had been for 22 years.

LISE MEITNER

Lise Meitner (1878–1968) was an Austro-Swedish **physicist** and radiochemist. She worked in Berlin with a German physicist named Otto Hahn (1879–1968). She was a Jew, and in the late 1930s she left Germany and settled in Sweden. In 1939, Hahn announced their joint discovery of nuclear fission. In this, the **nucleus** of the uranium **atom** fissions, or splits, into two smaller nuclei. These can go on to cause more fission in a chain reaction. Meitner refused to work on the atomic bomb and did no more work on nuclear fission. In 1960, she retired to England after living for 22 years in Sweden.

Later Life

In his later life, Einstein continued with his political work and the peace movement. He had become a U.S. citizen in 1940, while still keeping his Swiss nationality. He was always grateful to the U.S. for the warm welcome he had received when he fled **Nazi** Germany in 1933. But his peace and justice campaign after the war made him unpopular with the American authorities. He championed the public's right to know about the important issues of the day, such as whether nuclear weapons were being made. He also believed that teachers should be allowed to discuss these matters with their students without fear of censorship.

Investigations

During the 1950s, Einstein was suspected of having **communist** sympathies and was investigated by the **FBI.** He now began to campaign against the persecution of people suspected of having links with communists and of being involved in "un-American activities." Many of his friends and scientific colleagues were among those being investigated, including J. Robert Oppenheimer, who had been in charge of the Manhattan Project and was now Director of the **Institute for Advanced Study** at Princeton.

At press conferences, Einstein was often asked about his scientific ideas, but many people were also interested in his political views.

The prospect of nuclear war caused Einstein to worry about the future.

EINSTEIN FOR PRESIDENT

Einstein's support for **Zionism** since the 1920s made him an extremely popular figure in the new state of Israel. He had been one of the founders of the Hebrew University in Jerusalem, which he had helped open in 1922. He was so famous and popular that, in 1952, he was invited to become President of Israel as a mark of gratitude for all he had done for the Jewish people. But Einstein wished to avoid the world of politics as much as possible. Einstein declined the invitation with the words: "I am deeply moved by the offer…and at once saddened… because I cannot accept it. All my life I have dealt with objective matters. Hence, I lack both the natural aptitude and the experience to deal properly with people and to exercise official functions."

Einstein continued with his scientific research and his fight for truth and justice until the very end. One day in April 1955, Einstein collapsed at home and was rushed to the Princeton hospital. His doctors believed he could be saved if he agreed to have an operation, but he replied, "I do not believe in artificially prolonging life." In the morning of April 18, he died. He was 76. Beside his bed was a paper covered with his latest scientific calculations. His friend Alice Kahler, writing to a relative, said: "The world has lost its best man, and we have lost our best friend. And it came so suddenly."

Einstein's Legacy

Images of Einstein such as this often occur in magazines, newspapers, and other media, representing the "face of science."

For much of his life, Einstein's fame was legendary. His achievements made him one of the greatest scientists ever. But as well as for his scientific genius, Einstein is also remembered today for his modesty and his courage in his fight for world peace. He believed passionately that scientists should be fully responsible for their work and play their part in the world around them.

The face of science

Einstein was one of the founders of modern **physics.** He was the first scientist since Sir Isaac Newton, 200 years earlier, to come up with new explanations of how the universe works. Newton believed in "absolute" space and time. Einstein showed that space and time are "relative" measurements, which can be different when different people do the measuring, and that there is no such thing as a "correct" measurement.

Today, Einstein's theories of relativity form the basis of modern science. The special theory was accepted after a few years, as it answered many of the questions that scientists were asking at that time. But the general theory took longer to be accepted because people then could not see its practical use. It was not until much later, in the 1960s, that new devices such as **particle accelerators** were able to test parts of the theory. In 1976, **laser** experiments between the earth and the moon supported the general theory.

The enormous impact that Einstein's discoveries have had on the world can be shown by the fact that his name and face alone have come to symbolize science throughout the world. In his later years, he was nearly as famous for his political campaigns as he was for his scientific research. But he himself regarded his scientific work as the most important, as it opened up some of the greatest secrets of our world and universe.

In J. Robert Oppenheimer's words:

"There was always with him a wonderful purity at once childlike and profoundly stubborn."

Huge modern particle accelerators are important tools for research in nuclear physics today.

Discoveries Since Einstein

In his later years, Einstein searched for a theory that in one mathematical equation would bring together **gravity, electromagnetism,** and many other kinds of forces. In this way, he hoped to open up the innermost secrets of the universe, to understand how it and everything in it works. Scientists today continue with his quest for one theory that connects, or unifies, everything. This is known as the "grand unification theory."

The origin of the universe

In 1927, Belgian astronomer Georges Lemaître used Einstein's general theory of relativity to propose that the universe was still expanding. He claimed that the universe must have grown out of a tiny point of energy that exploded, and out of which came space, time, and **matter.** This has become known as the "Big Bang" theory and is now seen as the best explanation for the origin of the universe. In 1964, two American astronomers, Robert Wilson and Arno Penzias, picked up faint radio noise from space. This is now thought to be the echo of the Big Bang. As new discoveries have been made in space, the Big Bang theory has been refined and modified.

This diagram illustrates the Big Bang theory. Since its creation more than ten billion years ago, the universe has been constantly expanding.

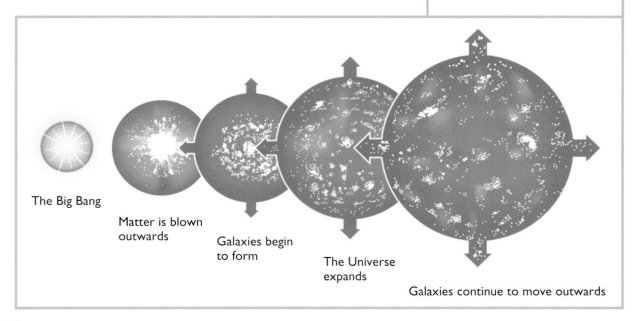

The Big Bang

Matter is blown outwards

Galaxies begin to form

The Universe expands

Galaxies continue to move outwards

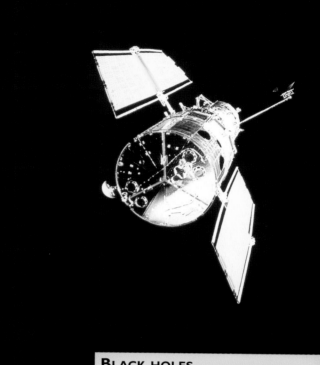

The Hubble Telescope was launched in 1993 to investigate our galaxy.

In 1970, British scientists Roger Penrose and Stephen Hawking proved that if Einstein's general theory of relativity is correct, then it is possible that there was a definite beginning to the universe. At this point, called a *singularity*, space and time as we know them would not have existed.

The future of the universe

In 1983, **physicists** used Einstein's general theory to work out the history of the universe back to a fraction of a second before the Big Bang. In 1993, the NASA satellite Cosmic Background Explorer (COBE) recorded the temperature of the afterglow of the Big Bang. Some scientists believe that in the far distant future, billions of years away, the universe could collapse in on itself and then be reborn in another Big Bang. Others believe that it will continue to expand until it fades away into a sea of **radiation.** But they are still inspired by Einstein in their search for a greater understanding of the universe.

BLACK HOLES

Using Einstein's general theory of relativity, astronomers have found extraordinary objects far away in space, such as **pulsars, quasars,** and black holes. In these situations, the force of gravity is extremely curved. A black hole occurs when matter becomes extremely dense, as in an exploded star. Around a black hole, the fabric of space-time is very curved. Its gravity becomes so strong that both matter and radiation, including light, are trapped inside.

Astronomers today are also looking for galaxies that might be acting as **"gravitational lenses."** Galaxies are much more massive than our sun and should therefore bend light rays even more than was predicted by Einstein and proved in 1919.

43

Timeline

1687	Sir Isaac Newton publishes his *Principia*.
1879	Birth of Albert Einstein in Ulm, Germany.
1887	Edward Morley and Albert Michelson demonstrate that the speed of light is constant.
1894	Einstein family moves to Milan, Italy.
1895	Albert joins his family in Milan and fails entrance exam for the Zurich Institute of Technology.
1896	Albert begins studying at the Zurich Institute.
1900	Max Planck introduces the idea of "quantizing energy."
1901	Einstein is granted Swiss citizenship.
1902	Begins work at the Bern **Patent** Office.
1903	Marries Mileva Maric, and daughter Lieserl is born.
1904	Birth of son Hans Albert.
1905	Einstein publishes three scientific papers, including one on his special theory of relativity.
1906	Writes his first paper on **quantum mechanics.**
1909	Resigns from the Patent Office and becomes an assistant professor at Zurich University, Switzerland.
1910	Birth of second son, Eduard.
1911	Marie Curie receives the **Nobel prize** for **physics** for her work on radioactivity, becoming the first person to win the prize twice. Ernest Rutherford shows that **atoms** have a central **nucleus.** Einstein is appointed Professor of Physics at the University of Prague.
1912	Becomes Professor of Physics at the Zurich Institute.
1913	Niels Bohr proposes a new model of the hydrogen atom.
1914	Einstein begins work as Research Director at the Institute of Physics in Berlin, Germany. He and Mileva separate and she moves back to Zurich with their sons. World War One begins.
1915	Einstein signs the Manifesto to Europeans, which calls for a league of nations to bring about peace.
1916	Publishes his general theory of relativity.
1918	World War One ends.
1919	Einstein and Mileva divorce. He marries Elsa Lowenthal. During a solar eclipse, Arthur Eddington successfully tests Einstein's general theory.

1922	Einstein is awarded the Nobel prize for physics for 1921. He also becomes a member of the League of Nations' Committee on Intellectual Cooperation.
1923	Edwin Hubble proves the existence of galaxies besides our own.
1927	Georges Lemaître proposes that the universe is continually expanding.
1929	Hubble shows that galaxies are moving away from each other.
1933	Adolf Hitler's **Nazi** Party comes to power in Germany. The Einsteins leave Europe and settle in the United States. Einstein begins teaching at Princeton University.
1936	Death of Elsa Einstein.
1937	Otto Hahn announces discovery, with Lise Meitner, of nuclear fission.
1939	World War Two begins. Einstein and other scientists write to President Roosevelt, urging him to develop an atomic bomb.
1940	Einstein becomes an American citizen, but keeps his Swiss nationality.
1941	United States enters the war.
1942	Manhattan Project to develop atomic bomb begins in the U.S. Enrico Fermi produces the first controlled nuclear reaction.
1945	First nuclear bombs dropped, on Hiroshima and Nagasaki in Japan. World War Two ends.
1948	The state of Israel is founded.
1952	Einstein is invited to become President of Israel.
1955	Albert Einstein dies in Princeton, New Jersey, at the age of 76.

More Books to Read

MacDonald, Fiona. *The World in the Time of Albert Einstein*. Parsippany, N.J.: Silver Burdett Press, 1998.

McPherson, Stephanie S. *Ordinary Genius: The Story of Albert Einstein*. Minneapolis, Minn.: Lerner Publishing Group, 1995.

Swisher, Clarice. *Albert Einstein*. San Diego, Calif.: Lucent Books, 1994.

Glossary

algebra branch of mathematics in which letters or other symbols are used to represent numbers

anti-Semitism persecution of or discrimination against people of Semitic origin, usually Jews

atom smallest particle of an element that has all its properties

botanist someone who studies plants

communist supporter of communism, the idea that there should be no classes in society and that no one should own anything privately

disarmament reduction by a country or a state of its weapons and armed forces

electromagnetic wave type of energy that includes gamma rays, X-rays, ultraviolet, visible light, infra-red, microwaves, and radio waves

electromagnetism magnetism produced by electric current

electron particle with a negative electric charge that orbits the nucleus of an atom

Fascism political movement started by Benito Mussolini in Italy that put nation and race before individuals and democracy

FBI (Federal Bureau of Investigation) branch of the Department of Justice that investigates the breaking of federal laws

gravitational lens object that has a strong gravitational pull

gravity force of attraction between any two objects that have mass

Institute for Advanced Study research institute in Princeton, New Jersey, founded in 1930

laser device for converting light of mixed frequencies into light waves of identical wavelength. A laser beam does not spread out like ordinary light waves and is therefore stronger.

mass amount of matter in an object

matter anything that occupies space and has mass

molecule smallest particle of a substance that normally exists on its own and still keeps its properties. Molecules usually consist of two or more atoms bound together.

Nazi member of the fascist National Socialist German Workers Party, which seized control in Germany in 1933

Nazism political creed followed by Nazis

neutral not taking part in a conflict, as a nation during wartime

Nobel prize prize for outstanding contributions to chemistry, physics, physiology or medicine, literature, economics, or peace

nuclear energy energy released during a nuclear reaction

nucleus central core of an atom, consisting of closely packed protons and neutrons

pacifist someone who believes that violence of any kind is unjustifiable, and that people should not take part in wars

particle minute amount of matter

particle accelerator machine for accelerating charged particles (protons and neutrons) to very high energies, used in nuclear physics to shatter atomic particles and provide information on their structure

patent government grant to an inventor, giving him or her the sole right to make, use, and sell their invention for a set period of time

physicist someone who studies physics

physics study of energy, matter, and their interactions

physiology branch of science dealing with the way living things, or organisms, function

pulsar very small star that rotates quickly, emitting pulses of radiation

quantum mechanics set of laws describing how atomic particles behave

quasar type of star that emits powerful radio waves and other forms of energy

radiation energy waves

socialist supporter of socialism, a political and economic system in which the government controls the means of production

species specific group to which a plant or animal belongs, within the larger genus or family group

Weimar Republic government that was founded in Germany in 1919 following the abdication of the Emperor

Zionism movement that supported the claims of Jews who felt that a Jewish homeland should be established in the Middle East

Index